2006

a morning cup of meditation™

Published by Crane Hill Publishers
www.cranehill.com

Printed in China

Library of Congress Cataloging-in-Publication Data

Bright-Fey, John A.
    A morning cup of meditation : one 15-minute routine to calm and cleanse your bodymind / by John A. Bright-Fey.
       p. cm.
    Includes bibliographical references and index.
    ISBN 1-57587-235-8 (alk. paper)
    1. Meditation.   I. Title.
BL627.B75 2005
158.1'2--dc22

2005012283

a morning cup of meditation

one 15-minute routine to calm
and cleanse your bodymind

john a. bright-fey

CRANE HILL
PUBLISHERS

Acknowledgments

I'd like to thank the following individuals for their invaluable help and advice. This morning cup would surely not taste as sweet without their assistance:

To all my students near and far who keep the campfires blazing in the New Forest;

To Professor Thomas Gibbs of Birmingham-Southern College and Professor Julie Steward of Samford University who bring the wonders of the contemplative life to their students;

To Ellen, Allison, and all the staff at Crane Hill Publishers for presenting me with this glorious opportunity;

To Charles Fechter, life-long friend and Boswell, for his continuing support during the writing and illustration process;

To Tim Rocks, Christena Brooks, and Miles Parsons for bringing the New Forest to life;

To my amazing wife, Kim, for all her love, energy, and support;

To all of you, much love and many thanks.

JB-F

This book is lovingly dedicated to my parents,
John and Dolores

Contents

"He whose joy is experienced within, whose pleasure and adventure are within, and whose imaginings and light are within, that devotee, being well established in the supreme kingdom, will attain absolute freedom."

The Song Celestial (*Bhagavad Gita*) (circa 500 BCE)

"Consciousness is the inner light kindled in the soul ... a music, strident or sweet, made by the friction of existence."

The Realm of Trust by George Santayana, American philosopher (1863–1952 CE)

Why Meditate?

I'm holding a thought, an idea, really, in my mind. What am I thinking? Let's see if you can guess what it is that I'm thinking about from these clues:

Doctors prescribe "it" for high blood pressure and heart disease (but "it" is not a drug).

Renowned scientists are working tirelessly to figure "it" out (but "it" is not a new discovery).

"It" helps you cope with anxiety, stress, and problems in your life (not a psychotherapist . . .).

"It" can dramatically enhance your self-esteem and appearance (... and "it" is cheaper than plastic surgery or a new car).

"It" boosts your insight, creativity, and overall intelligence (no, not a college course either).

Literally millions and millions of people take just a little of "it" every day for vibrant health and wellness (but "it" is not some kind of super-vitamin).

By now, I hope you're asking yourself, "What is this amazing *it*, and how can I get some?"

It is meditation, and the book you hold in your hands is all you need to set yourself on the road to boosting your immune system, reducing stress, and generally getting more out of life than you ever thought possible.

And how much time will you have to invest to get the benefits of this wonderful stuff? In the time it would take you to enjoy a cup of tea or coffee, you can reap the benefits of meditation and be solidly on the road to a happier and healthier lifestyle.

Juggling Life with Meditation 〰️

Do you ever feel as though you are out of step or out of tune with your life? Do you find yourself moving left when the events of a normally hectic day unexpectedly move to the right? Certainly each of us in a modern society learn how to juggle the many tasks that allow us to meet the demands of our busy lives. This, we are told, should bring us happiness and personal satisfaction. But no matter how skilled we are at juggling the day-to-day tasks that present themselves, we plainly do not feel good inside. Happiness and satisfaction become ephemeral. Worse still, at the end of our day, we often realize that we might have missed something really important: a child's accomplishment, a professional opportunity, a beautiful sunset, or a loved one in need of comfort.

Before drifting off to sleep to recharge our batteries, we promise ourselves that we *will* do better tomorrow; we'll be more optimistic and loving, more engaged and effective, more alert and aware.

Sometimes, we're able to keep this promise. Unfortunately, most often we aren't able to win the day as we had wanted, and the whole cycle begins again. Wouldn't it be great if you could break this cycle and get in tune with the song of your life? Well, that's why meditation was invented.

There are so many great reasons to meditate that it's hard to know where to begin any discussion of the subject. Surely our guessing game is a great place to start. People take up meditation to reduce stress, eliminate fatigue, and ease pain. They use it to cultivate inner peace and expand awareness, to reverse heart disease, and bolster the immune system. Meditation improves memory and concentration. It generates clarity of thought and quickness of mind. Athletes use it to boost their performance, and religious people use it to get closer to their god. It would take literally several volumes to present the latest scientific evidence that supports meditation, and more information keeps rolling in every day.

The regular practice of meditation promotes happiness and uncovers the individual source of bliss that lies within each of us. I really should say "play" instead of "practice," because meditation gets to be so much fun that you can't wait to play it. If this sounds good to you—and I hope it does—let me offer you a morning cup of meditation.

John Bright-Fey
Birmingham, Alabama
Spring 2005

Life Is a Symphony

Tuning Up

Meditation is a skill as old as humanity itself. Nearly every culture on planet Earth has discovered it in one form or another. But no matter what they have called it, meditation has become a way to tune up our minds and bodies—just like they were musical instruments. Think of it this way: life is a symphony, and your bodymind is an orchestra. And you, ultimately, should be the conductor of a finely tuned orchestra.

How do you know if your bodymind orchestra needs tuning up, so that you might better play the symphony of your life?

If you feel...
Stressed
Agitated
Angry
In pain
Confused
Whiny
Resentful
Empty
Tired all the time
Can't get a grip
Heartache
Uncomfortable
Can't think clearly
Grumpy
Afraid
Nervous
Edgy
Depressed
Pessimistic
Insignificant
—Then you need to meditate!

Can I Meditate? ~~~~~

You might think that a method that can so profoundly affect your life would be a rather complicated subject. But meditation isn't hard at all to understand—and it's even easier to do.

In reality, you already know how to meditate, but you might not "know that you know." When people tell me that they've never meditated, I ask them if they've ever loved anyone or anything before. "Of course," they say. Then I reply by telling them that love is a natural meditation.

As you have probably experienced at least once in your life, getting close to another person can often be a little bit scary. It can make you feel insecure and overly cautious. If you think about it too much, you can begin to obsess. Your obsessive over-thinking can even chase the other person away, or you could end up running away yourself. We do this because all of the things we think that *could* go wrong with a relationship—rejection, indifference, feigned affection, or the loss of individualism—might actually happen. In fact, our rational over-thinking mind is constantly reminding us of these grim possibilities.

But falling in love suspends the rational over-thinking mind so we can get past our fears and insecurities. Then we can truly connect with another human being. In doing so, we learn things *about* ourselves that we couldn't have possibly learned *by* ourselves. The "Love Meditation" allows us to feel the warmth and inspiration that comes from knowing that we are not alone.

That's what meditation is. It's a way to get past our fears, insecurities, past programming, bad habits, and old patterns of thinking and behaving, so we can get closer to life and closer to ourselves. Then we can hear our own sweet music and play out the symphony of our lives and loves.

New Forest Meditation

There are many different kinds of meditation. While each is designed for a specific purpose, some work better than others. Many once-effective methods have, over time, lost their focus. They have become overly complicated and obscured, or so imprinted with odd cultural doodads that they have been rendered ineffectual.

The meditative technique we will use is *New Forest Meditation.* This is my signature approach to the art and craft of meditation. I was introduced to meditation and contemplative prayer as a young and very religious child. It's important to understand that meditation and prayer are decidedly not the same thing. However, they complement each other completely, with one supporting the other. This drew me to a deeper exploration of many schools of meditation and contemplation. Eventually, I became a Meditation Master in several traditions, but all along the way, I was keenly aware of what was truly substantive and useful about each tradition and what was merely an element or facet from a culture and philosophy that was not native to me. I soon came to realize what was and was not relevant to modern life.

The happiness and health that meditation has brought me over the ensuing years has been, and continues to be, nothing short of amazing. Ever since I was a boy, I've wanted to share these wonders with everyone, regardless of age, religion, gender, or nationality.

My research and study in meditation was galvanized in the 1980s when I was hired to teach meditation, Tai Chi, and Qigong ("life-force yoga") to individuals who suffered from the aftereffects of strokes and traumatic brain injury. These people had no time to waste with foreign cultural trappings or airy philosophy. They needed the real benefits of meditation, and they needed them immediately. It was in this setting that the *New Forest Way* was born. Since then, I've used this same method with thousands of students with tremendous results.

New Forest eliminates all of the impediments and deficiencies that exist in other meditative methods. It also makes the wonders and benefits of the contemplative life available immediately to literally everyone. Now, one of the best kept secrets of the meditative world can be poured into your morning cup. Would you like a sip?

As New Forest meditators, we don't use words like "practice," "train," or "concentrate" to describe what we do. We say "play" instead. Lewis Carroll, the Victorian author of the classics *Alice in Wonderland* and *Jabberwocky*, created a word that describes the kind of play we engage in. His word is "galumphing," and it represents the activity of a child's game where the rules are few, but the pretend adventures are many. This is the kind of game we all used to play at one time in our life, but generally don't any more. A child is galumphing when a fallen stick becomes Excalibur and when a kitchen broom turns into a fiery horse.

As children, we played so we could explore the world around us, and in the process learn about our inner selves as well. When we played as children, we were refreshed, challenged, inquisitive, carefree, and happy. Play was an integral part of our health, growth, and development.

But as we grow up, the games get more serious and responsibilities become more adult. Our minds become less adventurous and less flexible. We often find ourselves stuck in habitual ways of thinking and behaving. Consequently, we stop exploring our deeper selves. It also becomes harder and harder to learn from our inner life, and when our heart speaks, we can barely hear it.

The only way to reclaim our minds, bodies, and our spirits is to learn to play again. Don't you think we could all stand to play a little every morning before we go out to meet the challenges of our day? I certainly think so. That's precisely what our meditation is designed for. It reintroduces us to the happy and unencumbered mind of the child that is in each of us.

The New Forest Language ~~~~~

When I was a child, I used to call prayer "talking with God."
But when I meditated, I called it "talking with my soul." The
imagination is the language of your soul, your deepest inner self. It
is your soul's Central Nervous System, the way it talks to you, and
you to it. Your mind with all its emotions is an important part of
your imagination. So are your memories.

I've always believed that your soul is constantly sending you all
of the wisdom and information you need to get the most out of any
situation you may encounter. It's constantly sending you feelings,
physical sensations, ideas, and mental images in an effort to
communicate with you. Our adult lives, though, can interfere with
this transmission and put static in the signal, garbling the incoming
soul messages. The meditation you're about to learn will start to

clear that signal up dramatically. But the problem of making sense of the soul's inner language still remains.

To solve that problem, all we need to do is play a game.

I first began using rhyming word-and-number games in childhood to help me remember how to perform the often complex mental gymnastics of Chinese and Tibetan meditation. I would twist and bend short poems and nonsense rhymes in my mind so that I'd have a way to easily translate old Chinese meditation instructions and ideas into a form I could easily remember. After all, to an American child, most of these ideas and concepts weren't culturally relevant; they came from Asian philosophy. They, simply put, were not meaningful to me. But the poems, rhymes, and number games gave me a basic structure to relate to. Eventually, I could use them to explain any meditative activity, no matter how detailed or complicated. My teachers said that it allowed me to get more deeply inside the inner world of meditation than any other student they'd ever seen.

As I worked to master Chinese art, poetry, movement, and philosophy, I created other mnemonics, including numbering and rhyming games, to help me comprehend their depths as well. Again, I used numbers to connect the internal secrets and philosophical roots of each exercise to its physicality. I also used these games to bring poetry and music to a physically expressive and deeply emotional level. Eventually, I infused meditation into everything I did.

Now, as a teacher, I use the same memory and number games to help my students. They find that their meditation is much easier to learn and more enjoyable to do. More importantly, the meaning and purpose of each meditative activity becomes almost instantly accessible—just as it did for me decades earlier.

The meditation that you are about to learn is easy and fun to do. You should have no trouble picking it up. But if you're to truly get in touch with your inner self, you need to learn the *New Forest* "1 through 10 Game."

The New Forest
"1 through 10 Game" ∿∿∿

If you can count from 1 to 10, you can meditate. It's as easy as that. The *New Forest* "1 Through 10 Keywords" will introduce you to the steps of your new meditation. Start by reading the following list aloud.

NUMBER	KEYWORD
1	Fun
2	Shoe
3	Tree
4	Core
5	Alive
6	Thick
7	Heaven
8	Gate
9	Shine
10	Spin

Now close your eyes and count from 1 to 10, saying the numbers and their keywords from memory. Recite silently or aloud; you choose. If you get stuck, open your eyes and read the list again—until you know all of the keywords and their associated numbers. It won't be long before you have easily memorized them. Each keyword will tell you what to think about as you meditate. They introduce you to ten carefully chosen visualizations that I call Internal Adjustments, because they subtly alter and adjust your focus on the inner landscape of your bodymind. It's as if each keyword represents a different part or section of your internal meditative orchestra. When you rest your mind on a keyword and its associated images, it tunes up that section! By the time you get to the last step, you'll be playing a symphony of soul music that will overflow from your inner to your outer world, bringing harmony wherever you go.

Shortly, during the Meditation Routine, you will learn the internal adjustment for each of the New Forest keywords. Although you'll be thinking about the "1 through 10" internal adjustments when you meditate, you can also think about them any time you see a number or group of numbers and bring the wonders of meditation to your everyday life. Once you get comfortable with the internal adjustments, you can project them into anything you do. Whether it's painting, sculpting, gardening, or mowing the lawn, any human activity can be transformed into a meditation by infusing it with ever-increasing levels of 1 through 10. Remember, you will be using these visualizations to tune up your inner orchestra so you can play your personal song and have a greater experience of the outside world.

Before they became mathematics, numerals themselves were considered to be magical. Indeed, the use of numbers in scientific calculations do effect great change in the modern world around us. But ancient man felt that simply thinking about them in the proper way (or given order) would cause beneficial change to the outside world. Now, with the "1 through 10 Game," they can be magical again as you use them to talk with your soul and create health and wellness within your inner world.

Meditative Posture:

Meditation can be done in almost any posture. It's only important at this stage to be as comfortable and balanced as possible. Here is the *New Forest* meditative posture.

Sitting Posture

Sit as upright as you can comfortably.

Eyes closed or open.

Breathe through your nose if possible.

Put a smile on your face!

Rest your relaxed hands on your legs or in your lap.

Feet flat on the ground, please.

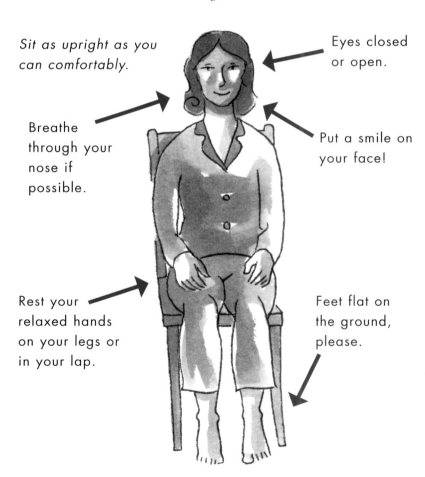

Sitting Posture

Gently droo
your shoulders.

Gently tuck in
your chin.

Support your
lower back.
Use a pillow
here if
necessary.

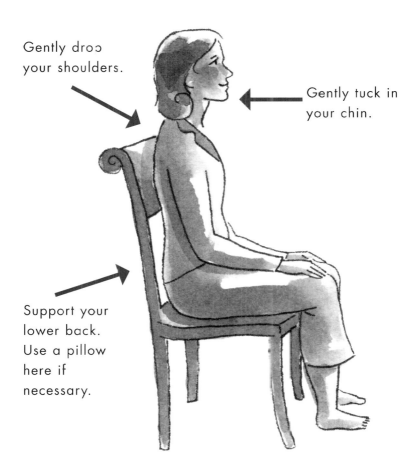

*Try to be centered and balanced
as you sit. Avoid slump'ng over or
leaning one way or the other.*

Meditative Breathing ~~~

The breath carries a special human signal with it that fixes whatever you are doing in emotional space and time. Said another way, it makes whatever you're doing more real and more authentic.

Some meditation methods rely on specialized and complicated ways of breathing, but not *New Forest*. Our goal is to relax as we breathe, returning to the unencumbered breath of a child at play. We accomplish this, as you might guess, by playing a game.

The balloon, glass tube, and thread game

Imagine that there is a balloon in your lower abdomen, located about 3 to 5 inches below your navel and inward, hidden deep inside you. As you breathe in, imagine that the inhaled air goes straight down to this balloon. As you breathe out, imagine that the balloon collapses. Did you notice that I did *not* say,

"… imagine that the balloon *contracts*"? This is very important. You are pretending that the air moves into and out of your bodymind of its own accord. The air simply comes into your balloon, expanding it to about the size of a grapefruit, and then leaves the balloon, which collapses as you exhale.

When you have a good sense of the balloon, imagine that there is a long glass tube that extends from the top of your balloon, straight up through the center of your torso and neck. Visualize the opened end of the glass tube pointing upward deep inside the center of your skull.

Imagine that the open end of this tube is where your breathing actually begins. Your nostrils are merely two holes conveniently placed to allow the air you breathe to get to the top of the open glass tube inside your head.

To complete the image, see the air that moves in and out of your bodymind as finely spun threads. Some *New Forest* meditators pretend that these threads are thin filaments of silver and gold. But whatever you envision, suggest to yourself that the gossamer threads of air are breathing you, as it were, rather than you breathing them. It's as if the air has a mind of its own and moves in and out of you of its own accord. Your job is to calmly watch it happen.

Over time, this way of breathing will change your relationship to precisely how you breathe. Your breath will naturally slow down, and your whole body will relax as your respiration becomes more efficient. Your blood will become filled with life-giving oxygen and energy. Every so often during your meditation, remember the "balloon, glass tube, and thread game." As you gain more facility with it, you'll find that you have greater control over your meditation. Soon everything that you do will become increasingly more comfortable.

Now that we know how to sit and breathe, we're almost ready to begin our meditation. But before we can begin, I have one more very important secret to tell you.

The Secret of the New Forest ∿∿∿

One of the most important secrets of *New Forest* meditation is the *New Forest* itself. Imagining yourself meditating in a beautiful natural setting has a profoundly nourishing effect on your entire bodymind and spirit. The outdoors is, after all, where we take vacations to recharge our batteries. At the turn of the twentieth century, physicians regularly prescribed time in nature as a foundation for curing most any illness. Photographs and paintings of nature fill us with awe and inspire us, because they remind us of our beginnings. Returning to the forest is a root experience for anyone human.

The ancient creators of meditation from around the globe used the wonders of the natural world as the primary source of their inspiration. I've always loved the word "inspired." It means "in spirit." As you meditate, you are playing in the spirit of the natural world, in fact, in the spirit of all creation. While it's always enjoyable to meditate outdoors, rarely is it convenient or practical. But envisioning the *New Forest* is something that you can do at any time, no matter where you are.

Think of the *New Forest* as an actual place that exists in a dimension parallel to your everyday world; it's always there—it always has been. It is your meditative refuge and sanctuary. You have just to think about it for it to appear. Our meditation forest is a lush, verdant environment teeming with life and energy. Growth and the hidden promise of growth exist all around you. Whatever you need for survival, nourishment, health, and wellness is waiting for you in the *New Forest*. As soon as you bring this forest into focus, all of the tools and materials you need to be at your best will present themselves to you.

To me, the *New Forest* represents a return to the Garden, a return to the field of all possibilities, where you can rest comfortably in God's hands. This is the ideal place to play your *New Forest* meditation.

The Meditation Routine

Find a quiet place to take your morning cup, a quiet corner in your favorite room, your back porch, even a peaceful garden. Place yourself in a comfortable seated position. You can be seated in a chair or on the floor in a cross-legged posture with cushions beneath you. It's your choice.

Stretch up with the top of your head. Find a point of balance and personal equilibrium, a still, central place from which to meditate. Relax and take a deep breath. Take another deep breath, long and deep to help clear your mind.

Let your mind and body quiet down, and visualize the *New Forest*. Here is the perfect place to completely rest and heal yourself. This forest is so beautiful, so peaceful; it's the most magnificent and comforting setting in the whole world. This is the place you come to reclaim yourself. This is the place where you can be who you really are. It is your private vacation spot far away from worries, discomfort, or pain. Just being here makes you feel better. In the *New Forest,* anything is possible.

Take another deep breath. Breathe in the wonders of the most beautiful natural setting in the whole world.

Number 1: The Keyword Is Fun

1. Put a faint smile on your face. Tell yourself to relax all over.

2. Every time you breathe out, imagine that invisible smiles are floating down through your bodymind. Wherever your imaginary smiles go, they help you feel more relaxed, comfortable, and warm. If you notice any tension, discomfort, or pain in your bodymind, just exhale and send a smile in that direction. Then suggest to the uncomfortable area that it, too, can relax and enjoy the moment.

3. As you let smiles float downward, suggest quietly to yourself that you will get more out of every aspect of your life if you smile and relax just a little bit more.

4. Take a deep breath by first inhaling. Now exhale, and let smile energy float downward through your body, relaxing every part of you that it touches.

Remember: Number 1, the keyword is Fun.

Extra Attention

During 1-Fun, your bodymind naturally relaxes downward as you breathe out. You can use this natural sensation to intensify the first internal adjustment. Every so often, imagine that one large smile amid the little ones slides down the front of your bodymind while you're exhaling. Tell yourself that this big smile deeply relaxes everything that it touches on its way down. Of course, since it's bigger, it relaxes you more. After sending a single big smile down the front of your bodymind, exhale and send one down your back. Feel it relax your neck, spine, and lower back. Use your imagination to see it move through the backs of your legs on its way to the backs of your feet and the floor. Then, at your next convenient exhale, send a huge Cheshire Cat grin down through the center of your bodymind. See it move through your lungs and chest, downward through the deepest parts of your bodymind, relaxing your bones, joints, and internal organs. Wherever this 1–Fun smile goes, tell yourself that it brings healing warmth, smile energy, and deep relaxation with it. It washes away tension and cleanses every part of you that it touches.

~

You can keep breathing smile energy downward for as long as you'd like. One or two minutes of big and little smiles relaxing you is enough to get the ball rolling. As a *New Forest* meditator, you want to spend time playing each internal adjustment from the first to the tenth. Remember: it's your job to tune-up and cleanse the entire bodymind. But if you feel extra-tense, go ahead and tarry at 1–Fun for a while. After all, you're the conductor of the orchestra; you can do whatever you want.

Number 2: The Keyword Is Shoe

1. Think about your feet and your toes inside your shoes—that is, if you're wearing any. If not, simply think about your feet and the ground beneath them. In fact, suggest to yourself that your feet are stuck to the ground.

2. Silently tell yourself that every time you exhale, the molecules of your feet blend in with the molecules of your shoes and the floor beneath them. The magnetic bonds that hold the atoms together loosen so that everything can intermingle. You don't know where your feet end and your shoes and the floor begin.

3. Take a deep breath. Go ahead, take another. Breathe out.

4. Feel your feet relax, and pretend that they are sinking into the floor. If you are lying down or sitting cross-legged, imagine that wherever your body rests, with every exhale, it sinks deeper into its resting place.

Extra Attention

Use whatever you can inside your imagination to suggest to yourself that your feet really are blending in with the floor. For example, see yourself standing barefoot in the mud after a warm summer rain. See it, feel it, taste it, and touch it with your imagination. Gently wriggle your toes and pretend that you can feel them squish deeper and deeper into the warm mud. Or you might pretend that your feet are ten times bigger and heavier than they normally are. You might even imagine that your shoes are made of iron, or that you have just realized that some practical joker has glued you to the chair and floor! Go ahead and chuckle lightly to yourself. Don't you remember that the 1–Fun smiles were just here?

Remember: Number 2, the keyword is Shoe.

Number 3: The Keyword Is Tree

1. Imagine that you are a huge tree with massive branches full of leaves and roots penetrating deeply into the soil. These roots grow to a depth twice your standing height, rooting you firmly into the planet. Every time you breathe out, your roots grow a few more inches deeper in to the soil.

2. Take a deep breath. Exhale and grow your roots a little deeper. As those roots grow and as your root system becomes more complex, your posture becomes more solid and firm. You are anchored so firmly that no wind or storm could ever uproot you. These same roots not only give you stability, they also draw nourishment from the earth. Feel this nourishment flow to every part of your bodymind as you breathe in and breathe out.

3. With every breath, draw vital nourishment into your bodymind through your roots. You also draw nourishment from the air through the smallest leaves (your fingers), through the branches (your hands and arms), and through the trunk (your body).

4. You are breathing the way trees breathe, purifying the air in the New Forest. You are a tree, living, growing, and healthy.

Remember: Number 3, the keyword is Tree.

Extra Attention

Find a tree, real or imaginary. This could be a painting or other representation of one. This will be the tree you will imagine yourself to be. Some New Forest meditators actually keep a picture of their tree in their journal or hanging on their wall. This serves as a constant reminder of the third internal adjustment. A little research will give you more information about trees, such as detailed pictures of their root structures and how they get water and minerals from the soil. My favorite tree was the one I played around as a child. It was a huge Chinese Elm that stood taller than our old two-story Southern home. Whenever I think 3-Tree, I see my old friend and remember all of the wonders I discovered growing up beneath its protective watch and ward. Even now, well into middle age, I can still touch its bark, smell its fragrance, and feel its tree wisdom in my mind. When I meditate, I fuse with those memories, and I become the elm.

Now it's time for you to make a 3-Tree memory of your own.

Number 4: The Keyword Is Core

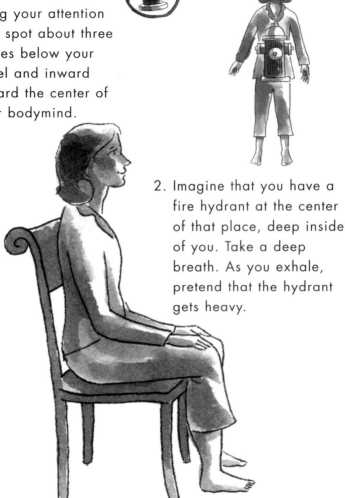

1. Bring your attention to a spot about three inches below your navel and inward toward the center of your bodymind.

2. Imagine that you have a fire hydrant at the center of that place, deep inside of you. Take a deep breath. As you exhale, pretend that the hydrant gets heavy.

3. Every time you breathe out, it gets heavier and heavier. With every exhalation, the image becomes more defined. The fire hydrant becomes heavier and more solid. Do whatever your imagination suggests to help you realize this image. Paint it your favorite color. Put your name on it. Imagine yourself sitting on it. This imaginary fire hydrant gives you an internal point of focus, a place to safely collect and condense your strength, a place to gather your thoughts.

4. Take a deep breath. This is your point of central focus. It is a source of immense energy that you can call upon whenever you need to strengthen anything or everything that you do.

Extra Attention

The area where your fire hydrant manifests itself is very important. Its placement is tied to very ancient rules for proper meditation. That having been said, you can shift your point of focus from your lower abdomen to other areas inside your bodymind if need be. For example, if you have a headache or a stomach ache, it's a better idea to place your imaginary heavy hydrant just underneath your breast bone. Women meditating during their menstrual cycle should place their 4–Core in this area as well.

Remember: Number 4, the keyword is Core.

Number 5: The Keyword Is Alive

1. Take a deep breath and focus inward.

2. Imagine that from your 4–Core fire hydrant you have fire hoses that run to your arms and legs. In fact, pretend that your arms and legs are those hoses and that your hands and feet are high-pressure nozzles. In addition, suggest to yourself that your hydrant-point-of-focus is connected to an invisible source of highly pressurized water or energy or life-force.

3. Take a deep breath. As you exhale, turn on your 4-Core fire hydrant and let its pressurized water energy rush at an incredible rate of speed through the hoses connected to it and out of your hands and feet into your surroundings. This is life-giving water. It is the energy that keeps all of us alive. See it, feel it, taste it, and touch it with your imagination. Hear it as it rushes from its gathering point (your 4-Core) through the pathways of your arms and legs and out your hands and feet. Do whatever you can with your imagination to help yourself really believe that this is happening. Extend life-force energy out into the world.

Remember: Number 5, the keyword is Alive.

Extra Attention

When you extend your energy outward through your arms and legs, you'll also be drawing life-force into your bodymind. Even though you're letting your mind rest on the image of extending water and energy, you will become a conduit of life-force. You have access to the power of the natural world, and that power flows through you as you play 5-Alive.

~

Now is a good time to remind you that playing each internal adjustment for a minute or two is sufficient to benefit fully from the meditation. But as I've already said, if a number and its image speaks to you in some way, spend a little extra time playing it. Remember, your soul is, at all times, sending you all the information you need to make the best possible decisions for yourself. You just have to listen.

Number 6: The Keyword Is Thick

1. Take a deep breath and close your eyes. Pretend that the air all around you is not empty space, but rather a thick, viscous liquid.

2. Imagine that you are sitting in a room filled with this unusual stuff. This liquid is so thick that you could relax completely and your bodymind wouldn't move, because the air itself is holding you in place, gently cradling you, and keeping you safe and secure. This thick air connects you to every part of the room and everything in it. It also connects you to everyone around you, and it integrates you completely with your surroundings.

3. Through the medium of this thick air, you will sense and feel anything that enters your environment. The air is so palpable and dense, if someone in the room were to move, you'd know it. The energetic vibrations of their movement will be transmitted to you through the thick air. Even your own movements would ripple through this thick air to every part of the room around you. It's as if you are sitting in the center of an energy web that stretches out in every direction.

Remember: Number 6, the keyword is Thick.

Extra Attention

You can supercharge this internal adjustment by suggesting gently to yourself that the thick air lets you feel or sense things that are out of the range of your sight. It's as if the web of thick air energy allows you to see around corners and behind furniture. When you play 6–Thick, you can also try to hear all around yourself, as if the viscous fluid acts as an inner radar. Imagine that this radar allows you to experience wherever you are omnidirectionally. With the sixth internal adjustment, you are supported and connected to the wonders of the world around you.

Number 7: The Keyword Is Heaven

1. Suggest to yourself that you are, ever so gently, being pulled upward toward the sky. The crown of your head (the highest part of your skull) is being pulled upward by some kind of benevolent and invisible connection.

2. As the crown of your head is lifted gently up, your chin may tuck in just a bit. Your neck and spine will relax downward, and you'll feel a little like a marionette. In your meditative pose, imagine that you are suspended between everything that is above you and everything that is below you: the wonders of the universe above you, the miracles of the earth below.

3. Take a deep breath as you breathe out, feel a gentle force tugging you upward, reminding you to maintain a light and sensitive feeling at the crown of your head. It feels as if your head wants to disengage from your neck and shoulders and float up into the sky. Think about what matters most in your life, your hopes, and your dreams. Let your mind rest on a religious image or a statement of faith if it's meaningful to you to do so. A short prayer is appropriate, or a silently wished "peace" for the world around you.

Remember: Number 7, the keyword is Heaven.

Extra Attention

3-Tree is a reminder of your terrestrial connection; that is, your intimate connection with the planet and your dependence on it. 7–Heaven reminds you that you are celestially connected as well, part of the limitless field of all possibilities that is God's universe, however you conceive it to be.

While *New Forest* meditation is decidedly nondenominational, playing it regularly promotes and nurtures a heartfelt reverence for what each of us recognizes as divine and godly. It not only reminds us of what is right with the world, but also intuitively reveals to us ways in which we can help make it a better place. This sounds like heaven to me.

Number 8: The Keyword Is Gate

1. Pretend that every pore of your skin is a tiny doorway or gate. Take a deep breath.

2. As you inhale, suggest to yourself that you are not just breathing with your nose, but through every pore of your skin. It's as if every pore—a tiny gate—swings open to draw nourishing air into it as you breathe in.

3. As you breathe out, the gates close, and the life-giving oxygen that you've inhaled through your skin moves around inside you, penetrating every muscle and vein and condensing around every bone and joint. Everywhere this air goes, it heals and repairs; it relaxes and smoothes; it stimulates growth and releases pain.

4. Open the gates and breathe in close the gates and let the air move around inside you. It may be helpful to see the air as visible matter, perhaps made up of the tiny silver and gold threads. When you inhale, the gates open wide, and the tiny silver and gold threads are absorbed into your  bodymind through each and every pore. Then, as you begin to exhale, the 8–Gate doors close, and all of those tiny silver and gold threads swirl around inside your bodymind and cascade over your bones, muscles, and organs, bringing life-giving oxygen and healing energy to every part of your bodymind. If you are experiencing pain in any specific area, send extra silver and gold threads to it. You can will energy to any site that needs healing. You breathe in this healing energy with every breath you take. The entire surface of your bodymind breathes in nourishing and life-giving air.

Remember: Number 8, the keyword is Gate.

Extra Attention

This internal adjustment helps eliminate any unhealthy barriers separating you from the love, power, wisdom, and knowledge of the world around you. It's as if you're spreading your arms wide and giving the world a big hug. Breathe in and open your arms in your imagination, then breathe out and visualize yourself completing the embrace.

~

I tend to play 8–Gate a bit longer than the other internal adjustments because it feels so good! Just breathe normally and gently match the breath to the "open–absorb" and the "close–condense." Remain as comfortable as possible. Try not to control your breathing. Suggest gently to yourself that it would be nice if your breathing was relaxed, unhurried, and unworried.

Number 9: The Keyword Is Shine

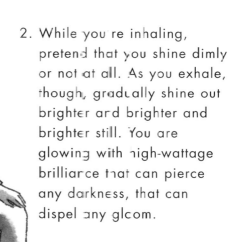

1. Imagine you are a human-sized light bulb. Take a deep breath. As you inhale, imagine that potential energy enters your body through every pore, just as the silver and gold threads did in the 8–Gate meditation.

2. While you're inhaling, pretend that you shine dimly or not at all. As you exhale, though, gradually shine out brighter and brighter and brighter still. You are glowing with high-wattage brilliance that can pierce any darkness, that can dispel any gloom.

3. This is your activity: inhale and gradually get dimmer; exhale and shine outward at a dazzling intensity.

4. Would you rather be a bright candle flame or brilliantly glowing golden flower? It is your choice. Use all of your imaginative powers to make this visualization real. When you exhale, shine brightly. When your intellect penetrates to the core of a problem and solves it, a burst of energy is released throughout your bodymind. This moment of discovery signals an unusual clarity of intellect and an elevation of mood. Your whole bodymind seems to glow with exhilaration. When you imagine yourself shining outward, your mind will focus and your spirits will brighten.

Remember: Number 9, the keyword is Shine.

Extra Attention

It's this simple: positive thoughts have a good effect on our entire organism, and negative thoughts affect us badly. The ninth internal adjustment generates and supports thoughts of well-being that elevate the entire bodymind; *i.e.*, it helps you feel great! 9–Shine establishes ease where dis-ease was before.

Cheerfulness and optimism are hallmarks of *New Forest* meditators. With every exhalation, you shine out brightly, and in doing so, you connect peacefully and cheerfully with the world around you. 9–Shine also helps you establish an abiding sense of peace within yourself that makes you feel happy and healthy. With all of this going on, you can't help but smile.

~

At times, separating the 8–Gate image from the 9–Shine image can be difficult. They fit nicely together, don't they? My advice is to let them play together as much as they want. After all, 9 follows 8 for a reason. But remember: you are the conductor; you are in charge. It's important that you have a simple, direct, and separate experience for each of the nine internal adjustments we've done so far. Don't worry though; in a short time, you'll be able to conduct your internal orchestra with ease.

Number 10: The Keyword Is Spin

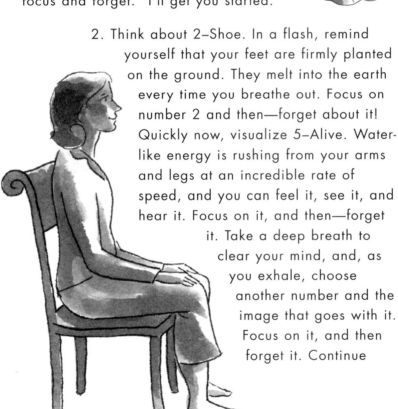

1. Let the first nine numbers and their associated images come to you in any order. When meditating in the New Forest, we call it "focus and forget." I'll get you started.

2. Think about 2–Shoe. In a flash, remind yourself that your feet are firmly planted on the ground. They melt into the earth every time you breathe out. Focus on number 2 and then—forget about it! Quickly now, visualize 5–Alive. Water-like energy is rushing from your arms and legs at an incredible rate of speed, and you can feel it, see it, and hear it. Focus on it, and then—forget it. Take a deep breath to clear your mind, and, as you exhale, choose another number and the image that goes with it. Focus on it, and then forget it. Continue

selecting numbers in any order and keep it up for as long as you'd like. Focus on first one number and its image, and then another. Let the images arise as randomly as possible. However they present themselves, watch with a casual attention.

3. The secret to this tenth meditation is to get the other nine numbers and their internal adjustments gently spinning at the same time. This is not automatic at first, but eventually it will happen, and you will become a juggler, balancing one meditation skill with another.

Remember:
Number 10, the
keyword is Spin.

Extra Attention

New Forest meditation is purposefully open and flexible so you can bend and shape it, making it as personal as you'd like. The details of each internal adjustment are left up to you. They must come from your experience and your imagination. The more personal the adjustments are, the deeper their effect on you.

With the tenth internal adjustment, you allow your intuition to tell you what number you should think about. After all, your deepest self knows what you need in order to accomplish your wellness goals. So why not let it speak to you in the language of *New Forest* numbers, the ideas, and sensations associated with each? For example, if you really need to be relaxed, 1–Fur will bubble to the surface. If 7–Heaven appears, then it's time to take notice, stretch up a bit, and muse about your higher aspirations. Then, right in the middle of your lofty thoughts, you realize, "Golly! I can't feel my '3-Tree' roots. I wonder what made me think about that." It really doesn't matter. Simply focus on 3-Tree for a few breaths and look within to see which number next presents itself to you.

~

In addition to openness and flexibility, *New Forest* is also designed to be radically inclusive and nonjudgmental. Do not draw any conclusions as to why a given number presents itself to you. 10–Spin is, after all, about slipping past the rational thinking mind and developing an intuitive relationship with the inner self that is your soul. Any thought is allowed; don't judge them. Merely interpret each one in the language of *New Forest*. Let it speak to you in the language of images, memories, energy, physical sensations, and number shapes. Every thought and sensation has its own energy. Soon, you will learn to sit comfortably with each as you conduct your inner symphony.

Closing Your Meditation

Let's close our meditation. I want you to count down from 10 to 1: 10–Spin, 9–Shine, 8–Gate, 7–Heaven, 6–Thick, 5–Alive, 4–Core, 3–Tree, 2–Shoe, 1–Fun.

Relax and rest peacefully with your meditations. Allow the image of the *New Forest* to slowly fade away. Don't worry though; it's there any time you need to take a morning cup of meditation.

Questions and Answers:
A Meditator's Guidebook

Q: How often should I meditate?

A: This is entirely up to you. Once a day, twice a day, three times a week—you choose what works best for your busy schedule. I personally prefer the once-a-day plan. Eventually, sitting in meditation will become so enjoyable that you'll hardly be able to wait until the next session.

Q: I don't have time to meditate. What can I do?

A: To that I can reply only that I myself don't have time to be nervous, stressed out, disorganized, unhappy, sick, or pessimistic. That's why I make time to meditate.

Q: Is sitting in a chair the only posture I can use while I'm meditating?

A: No, it isn't. There are many different *New Forest* meditative postures, each with its own effects and focus. Sitting upright in a chair is certainly the best way to receive all-around benefit for the bodymind. But you can flavor your morning cup by occasionally choosing one of these postures:

1. Sit cross-legged on the floor to concentrate life-force energy in and around your internal organs as you meditate.

2. Lie on your back for profound deep relaxation.

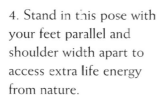

3. Gently hold this posture (which is called the "Universal Post") to build physical strength and determination.

4. Stand in this pose with your feet parallel and shoulder width apart to access extra life energy from nature.

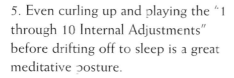

5. Even curling up and playing the "1 through 10 Internal Adjustments" before drifting off to sleep is a great meditative posture.

Q: Do I have to be still to meditate?

A: Absolutely not! In fact, any activity can be turned into a *New Forest* meditation. Here's how you do it:

1. Pick a normal everyday activity such as walking the dog, doing dishes, gardening, or mowing the lawn;
2. Visualize the *New Forest*;
3. Perform your activity in a deliberate and mindful way while ...
4. ... playing the "1 through 10 Internal Adjustments."

It's that simple. Any human task can be turned into a meditation by infusing it with ever-increasing levels of the *New Forest* "1 through 10." Think of sitting or standing still in meditation as a formal activity. Blending *New Forest* meditation with your day-to-day tasks can then become a more playful, or informal, practice.

Q: When I meditate, will I be emptying my mind?

A: I hope not! Inexperienced meditators often use this phrase to describe how their minds feel when they start to tune them up. Usually, our minds are filled with all kinds of random, unorganized thoughts, feelings, and emotions. I call these "small confusions." When you first begin to meditate, your whole bodymind gets very organized and the small confusions fade away. At first, this feels like the mind empties out and goes silent. It's as if the noisy children have finally drifted off to sleep. But over time, and as your skill at meditation deepens, you will become aware of more subtle layers of noise and mental activity. These, too, will become organized with repeated trips to the *New Forest*. We don't want to silence the orchestra or prevent them from playing. Rather, our goal is to eliminate the small confusions that stand between us and the enjoyment of the beautiful music of our lives.

Q: How can I avoid distracting thoughts when I meditate?

A: You can't—nor should you try to—avoid the distracting thoughts that bubble up during your "1 through 10" meditation. Mental distractions are part of being human, and you shouldn't let them get in your way. For example, pretend that you are in the middle of playing the fifth internal adjustment. Water energy is rushing out of your arms and legs. and, all of a sudden, you remember a phone call you should have made. As soon as you realize that you are thinking about the phone call—and not the 5–Alive fire hoses—smile, silently let yourself off the hook, and return to playing with the 5–Alive images. Distractions happen: don't worry about them. It's as easy as that.

Q: Is the goal of meditation to stop thinking?

A: No. The goal of meditation is to bring harmony to your thoughts and not to stop them altogether Experienced meditators know that organized and harmonious thinking driven by our higher ideals and aspirations are the keys to making our lives and our world a better place.

Q: Do I always have to use the CD to guide my meditation?

A: No. Use the accompanying audio CD until you can play the meditation on your own. Some people need to hear or read the instructions only once to absorb the meditation. For others, it takes several times. Everyone is different. I've found that once the images are "off the page," so to speak it helps to go back to the book every so often for a fresh reading. Doing so will supercharge your meditation for years to come.

Q: When will I be Enlightened?

A: Popular books and magazines on meditation talk a lot about Enlightenment, Illumination, and Sudden Awakening—too much, in my opinion. You will never step through an Enlightenment doorway, become One of the Great, and leave the rest of us and the dull world behind. That's as plain as I can say it.

Illumination experiences brought on by meditation can be very profound and life-transforming. The truth, however, is that real Enlightenment usually comes to us in small bites so that its wisdom can be easily assimilated into our daily lives. *New Forest* meditation is specifically designed to engineer a complete experience of life where, for example, you look at a rose and see its beauty and elegance as if you'd never seen one before. Fast food will taste like a gourmet meal, and when your child smiles, it will be like you're seeing it for the very first time. What could be more enlightening than that?

Q: Can I combine *New Forest* meditation with yoga, Tai Chi, or aerobics?

A: Sure! Why not? *New Forest* can be adapted to any exercise and wellness program to make it more effective. In fact, I've written two other books in the Morning Cup series that examine other branches of the *New Forest* tree. They are *A Morning Cup of Tai Chi* and *A Morning Cup of Qigong* (Qigong is "life-force Yoga"). As a unit, these three books form a dynamic approach to health and wellness that, in my humble opinion, is second to none.

An Extra Sip #1:
The Internal Adjustment Energies

At a normal pace, your meditation routine should take about 15 minutes to perform. That's about a minute and a half for each of the ten adjustments. But there isn't an optimal amount of time that is "best" for meditation. Fifteen minutes gets the job done, but five minutes works just as well. You can meditate longer, too. Play in the *New Forest* as long as you'd like.

While it's best to play all ten of your internal adjustments, sometimes it feels good to spend your Morning Cup time focusing on only three or four of them—or even just one. The question is "How do I know which one to choose?"

Each of the ten *New Forest* internal adjustments addresses a certain type of energy that we need in order to live life to the fullest. Each adjustment can mobilize and organize its specific energy when we need it the most. Advanced meditators even believe they can see the shape of the ten different energies as they move in and around the bodymind. The internal adjustments and their respective energies and shapes are:

1–Fun generates comforting energy
2–Shoe generates grounding energy
3–Tree generates nourishing energy
4–Core generates strengthening energy
5–Alive generates outflowing energy
6–Thick generates connecting energy
7–Heaven generates uplifting energy
8–Gate generates balancing energy
9–Shine generates protecting energy
10–Spin generates intuitive energy

Internal adjustment
1–Fun generates
comforting energy

Internal adjustment
2–Shoe generates
grounding energy

Internal adjustment
3–Tree generates
nourishing energy

Internal adjustment
4–Core generates
strengthening energy

Internal adjustment
5–Alive generates
outflowing energy

Internal adjustment
6–Thick generates
connecting energy

Internal adjustment
7–Heaven generates
uplifting energy

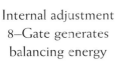

Internal adjustment
8–Gate generates
balancing energy

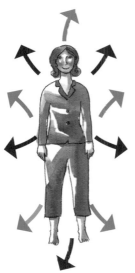

Internal adjustment
9–Shine generates
protecting energy

Internal adjustment
10–Spin generates
intuitive energy

At its simplest, knowing the name of each energy will tell you which one could most benefit you.

If you're feeling tense or uncomfortable, play adjustment 1—Fun and generate comforting energy.

Has the pace of life got you running around and feeling unstable? Then you need grounding energy, which is generated by focusing on 2—Shoe.

Feeling undernourished by life? Then play the 3—Tree and generate nourishing energy.

If you're feeling physically, intellectually, or emotionally weak, strengthen yourself with 4—Core.

Any time you use your hands to touch people or engage in a craft, you can dramatically increase their effectiveness by playing 5—Alive and generating abundant outflowing energy. (4—Core and 5—Alive played together are great for practitioners of the healing arts.)

From time to time, we all feel cut off from our environment and the people in it. This is an indication that we need more connecting energy. Play 6—Thick.

Play 7—Heaven whenever you need a clear head.

Balance out the conflicts and confusions in your life with internal adjustment 8—Gate, and protect yourself from negative emotions with 9—Shine, generating protective energy.

Boost your intuition and creativity with 10–Spin, and apply that kind of energy to whatever it is that you do.

Soon, throughout your day, you will start to intrinsically know which energy or energies need to be cultivated. Then you can make whatever internal adjustment is needed whether you're at the store, in your garden, or at the bank. Eventually, you will participate in an intimate conversation with your innermost self. Silent words, energy, feelings, and lush images will become a subtle language of nuance and profound import. In essence, you will be having a conversation with your bodymind. You'll be guided by your intuition, higher ideals, and innermost self—the soul.

An Extra Sip #2:
The Master's Secrets

The bulk of today's scientific research on meditation focuses on the areas of stress reduction, performance, and health and wellness. At the same time, "pop culture" writings on the subject tend to focus on lofty expressions of ultimate reality such as enlightenment, oneness, and transcendence. Between these two, the scientific and pop culture, lies a whole world of experience that almost never gets talked about; namely, how does regular life feel to regular people who meditate regularly?

Often, meditation masters will not talk openly about what happens to someone who steadfastly plays the meditations that they teach. This is a sad occurrence and has much to do with the cultures and traditions of eastern countries. Wouldn't it be great for you to know when your meditations are really working? Or how life will begin to feel when you've meditated over a long period of time?

I've always found that telling students what they're likely to encounter in their meditative travels provides them with an effective tool for judging how well their meditation is informing their lives. Don't expect to experience or feel these things all at once. Real skill in meditation accumulates in bits and pieces over time. Still, it's nice to know what life will feel like after you've been meditating for a long time.

In addition to the happiness and the health and wellness that come from being transformed by meditation, there can be many other sensations. When you've been meditating in the *New Forest* for a very long time, life feels as if it's unfolding slowly and deliberately, even when it would otherwise seem to be very hectic and fast-paced. Life appears to be amazingly delicate. This is a palpable sensation, something far more real that a mental image. This delicacy seems to be as real as gravity. Life feels as if you were to grasp or push it too hard, it might break. Yet, at the same time, it feels indestructible. After you've been meditating for a while, it feels as if you are somehow removed from the reality of life, yet you know you are very much a part of it. Each moment and each occurrence feels somehow strange, yet somehow familiar—and all you can do is observe each one. You feel completely indifferent to each moment and occurrence, no matter how pleasurable or offensive and no matter how subtle or profound. No one moment or occurrence is more or less important than any other. They are all informative, powerful, and life-affirming.

You experience each moment and occurrence completely. In fact, you feel as if you *are* each moment and occurrence. This feeling, this sense, arises from an all-encompassing reverence for what is transpiring before you. This is a quiet reverence, and you will hold it very gently, like a newborn infant in your arms. You will focus on it completely. The infant's heartbeat will become your own, and you will be completely alert to its shifts and movements.

You will feel as if each facet of your life—in fact, life itself—is a private conversation you are holding with yourself: every moment, every occurrence, and every person relates to you directly and addresses a need or a desire that is unique to you. Everything-that-is relates to you personally and is connected with you. Life speaks to you everywhere—to you and only you. You will feel as if each turn of your wrist and every one of your thoughts and actions changes the face of the world and shapes and reshapes the universe. This feeling is palpable and completely real. Your intent is solid and more real than physical action. The intent to drive a nail has far more force and power than the muscle, arm, and the aim of the descending hammer, and when you swing the hammer, you split worlds.

You feel as if you're living life in complete compliance with where you are and what's going on around you. Circumstances will seem to control you completely, yet, at the same time, you will feel as if you are in complete and constant control of everything. As you reach out and touch life, you are creating it, and simultaneously, life is creating you.

Amid the overwhelming power, force, and flow of life and all its events and moments, you will feel as if you are completely a public being, yet somehow totally alone. Each person—every little thing, thought, and occurrence—feels so finely important to you that each one can supersede anything else that is occurring. You are so intimately connected to the totality of life that even the smallest event becomes a miraculous occurrence. The purring of a cat can become your salvation, your key to heaven.

You feel astonished at everything; you are totally, gently awestruck. You see miracles everywhere, and you see miracles giving birth to other miracles. As waves of miracles move out in all directions, intersecting and colliding with other waves of miracles, they outline what you perceive to be the source of all miracles. They reveal the source of the miraculous. The ambiance that spreads throughout your bodymind at this revelation (itself also a miracle) is constant and all-encompassing. You identify yourself as part of the miraculous. You *are* a miracle.

You perceive every moment of life and every occurrence of life as universal and everlasting. It is as if a timeless, spaceless power and force continuously issue forth from a beatific yet undifferentiated place. These moments and occurrences come from the source, but you feel as if they issue forth from you as well, as if you yourself are the gatekeeper of all possibilities and all life. You also feel as if every moment and occurrence of life returns to the source through you. You become the point of egress and ingress for life. You feel as if life could not possibly occur without you at its portal. At the same time, you are its expression and could not possibly exist yourself unless it moved through you.

You feel as if life is completely impromptu, unfolding spontaneously, totally ephemeral. Every moment and occurrence is perceived as being completely isolated in space and time, existing only from the instant it appears until the time that it vanishes. You experience each beat of life—or of God's heart—as if it will never appear again. You feel as if you are constantly in the presence of a priest who is continually blessing you with power, love, and grace. Everything in nature and creation *is* a blessing. Though God is everywhere, it's as if God has an invisible emissary whose sole job is to carry God and all of God's gifts to you and the world around you. This living being, your angel and guide, acts effortlessly to accomplish this task.

Here is a vision of your future. Here is a description of what a *New Forest* meditator can feel. Who wouldn't want to experience life this way? The secrets—the keys to this complete experience of living—are already yours. Your "1 through 10 Meditation" has shown you a way to the fullest possible appreciation of living. The way is open before you. You have only to choose to continue.

The possibilities are infinite.

About the Author

John Bright-Fey is a 40-year veteran of the Chinese Health Exercise and Martial Arts. A highly accomplished Master Instructor, he is an expert and world-renowned authority on Tai Chi, Qigong, and meditation.

John moved to Alabama from California in 1990 with his wife, Kim, a licensed physical therapist and certified Kung-Fu instructor. A year later, he opened the Blue Dragon Academy in Hoover, Alabama, where he teaches Tai Chi and other Chinese disciplines.

His instructional video "New Forest Tai Chi for Beginners" consistently ranks among the top-selling videos in the country.